# STAR WARS

## THE FORCE AWAKENS

# MAD LIBS®

by Eric Luper

PRI
An Imprint

PRICE STERN SLOAN
Penguin Young Readers Group
An Imprint of Penguin Random House LLC

*Star Wars: The Force Awakens* Mad Libs © & TM 2016 Lucasfilm Ltd.

Mad Libs format copyright © 2016 by Price Stern Sloan,
an imprint of Penguin Random House LLC. All rights reserved.

Concept created by Roger Price & Leonard Stern

Published by Price Stern Sloan, an imprint of Penguin Random House LLC,
345 Hudson Street, New York, New York 10014.
Printed in the USA.

ISBN 9781101995488
1 3 5 7 9 10 8 6 4 2

# MAD LIBS

# INSTRUCTIONS

MAD LIBS® is a game for people who don't like games!
It can be played by one, two, three, four, or forty.

## ● RIDICULOUSLY SIMPLE DIRECTIONS

In this tablet you will find stories containing blank spaces where words
are left out. One player, the READER, selects one of these stories. The
READER does not tell anyone what the story is about. Instead, he/she asks
the other players, the WRITERS, to give him/her words. These words are
used to fill in the blank spaces in the story.

## ● TO PLAY

The READER asks each WRITER in turn to call out a word—an adjective or
a noun or whatever the space calls for—and uses them to fill in the blank
spaces in the story. The result is a MAD LIBS® game.

When the READER then reads the completed MAD LIBS® game to the other
players, they will discover that they have written a story that is fantastic,
screamingly funny, shocking, silly, crazy, or just plain dumb—depending
upon which words each WRITER called out.

## ● EXAMPLE (*Before* and *After*)

"_____!" he said _____
　　　　EXCLAMATION　　　　　　　　　　　　ADVERB

as he jumped into his convertible _____ and
　　　　　　　　　　　　　　　　　　　NOUN

drove off with his _____ wife.
　　　　　　　　　ADJECTIVE

"____OUCH____!" he said ____STUPIDLY____
　　　EXCLAMATION　　　　　　　　　　　ADVERB

as he jumped into his convertible ____CAT____ and
　　　　　　　　　　　　　　　　　NOUN

drove off with his ____BRAVE____ wife.
　　　　　　　　ADJECTIVE

# QUICK REVIEW

In case you have forgotten what adjectives, adverbs, nouns, and verbs are, here is a quick review:

An ADJECTIVE describes something or somebody. *Lumpy*, *soft*, *ugly*, *messy*, and *short* are adjectives.

An ADVERB tells how something is done. It modifies a verb and usually ends in "ly." *Modestly*, *stupidly*, *greedily*, and *carefully* are adverbs.

A NOUN is the name of a person, place, or thing. *Sidewalk*, *umbrella*, *bridle*, *bathtub*, and *nose* are nouns.

A VERB is an action word. *Run*, *pitch*, *jump*, and *swim* are verbs. Put the verbs in past tense if the directions say PAST TENSE. *Ran*, *pitched*, *jumped*, and *swam* are verbs in the past tense.

When we ask for A PLACE, we mean any sort of place: a country or city (*Spain*, *Cleveland*) or a room (*bathroom*, *kitchen*).

An EXCLAMATION or SILLY WORD is any sort of funny sound, gasp, grunt, or outcry, like *Wow!*, *Ouch!*, *Whomp!*, *Ick!*, and *Gadzooks!*

When we ask for specific words, like a NUMBER, a COLOR, an ANIMAL, or a PART OF THE BODY, we mean a word that is one of those things, like *seven*, *blue*, *horse*, or *head*.

When we ask for a PLURAL, it means more than one. For example, *cat* pluralized is *cats*.

MAD LIBS® is fun to play with friends, but you can also play it by yourself! To begin with, DO NOT look at the story on the page below. Fill in the blanks on this page with the words called for. Then, using the words you have selected, fill in the blank spaces in the story.

Now you've created your own hilarious MAD LIBS® game!

# THE FORCE AWAKENS

PLURAL NOUN _____

A PLACE _____

NOUN _____

ADJECTIVE _____

NOUN _____

VERB _____

PERSON IN ROOM _____

VERB ENDING IN "ING" _____

NOUN _____

NOUN _____

ADJECTIVE _____

ADJECTIVE _____

PLURAL NOUN _____

VERB _____

VERB _____

# MAD LIBS

# THE FORCE AWAKENS

It's been thirty _____ since the Battle of (the) _____ .
_____PLURAL NOUN_____                              _____A PLACE_____

Luke _____ -walker has vanished, and the _____
_____NOUN_____                                              ___ADJECTIVE___

First Order has risen from the ashes of the Galactic Empire. With the

_____ of Kylo Ren, the First Order will not _____
___NOUN___                                                          ___VERB___

until Skywalker has been destroyed. General Leia Organa, with the

help of Poe, Finn, Rey, BB-8, and _____ , is also searching
                                        ___PERSON IN ROOM___

for Luke in the hopes of _____ peace to the galaxy. BB-8
                            ___VERB ENDING IN "ING"___

has the _____ the Resistance needs to find Luke, but the
            ___NOUN___

droid has been stranded on the desert _____ of Jakku
                                            ___NOUN___

with only the help of _____ stormtrooper Finn and
                          ___ADJECTIVE___

the _____ scavenger Rey. Will the Resistance have the
       ___ADJECTIVE___

_____ to stop the First Order and _____ Luke?
___PLURAL NOUN___                                  ___VERB___

Or will the First Order _____ Luke before he ever has a
                            ___VERB___

chance to help?

From STAR WARS: THE FORCE AWAKENS MAD LIBS® • © & TM 2016 Lucasfilm Ltd.
Published by Price Stern Sloan, an imprint of Penguin Random House LLC, 345 Hudson Street, New York, NY 10014.

MAD LIBS® is fun to play with friends, but you can also play it by yourself! To begin with, DO NOT look at the story on the page below. Fill in the blanks on this page with the words called for. Then, using the words you have selected, fill in the blank spaces in the story.

Now you've created your own hilarious MAD LIBS® game!

## MEET BB-8

NOUN _____

NOUN _____

ADJECTIVE _____

NOUN _____

ADJECTIVE _____

NOUN _____

VERB ENDING IN "ING" _____

VERB _____

SAME VERB _____

ADVERB _____

PLURAL NOUN _____

ADJECTIVE _____

ADJECTIVE _____

VERB _____

PLURAL NOUN _____

NOUN _____

# MAD LIBS®

## MEET BB-8

Never before, in the history of _____ Wars, have we seen
                                    NOUN

an astromech droid shaped like a/an _____. Owned by
                                         NOUN

Poe Dameron, BB-8 rolls around fulfilling _____ missions
                                              ADJECTIVE

and helping the Resistance fight the First _____. Just
                                               NOUN

as _____ on the sand as he is on solid _____,
      ADJECTIVE                                      NOUN

BB-8 finds himself _____ across deserts and bouncing
                    VERB ENDING IN "ING"

around the *Millennium Falcon*. He can also _____ down the
                                                VERB

stairs. Just don't ask him to _____ back up! BB-8 also fits
                                SAME VERB

_____ into Poe's T-70 X-wing, *Black One*, helping him pilot
   ADVERB

in _____ and performing _____ repairs. When
    PLURAL NOUN                       ADJECTIVE

Rey meets BB-8, she knows he's _____. Even though she is
                                   ADJECTIVE

offered a lot of portions for BB-8, she decides to _____ him.
                                                       VERB

And BB-8 *is* special. Not only does he have the _____ to
                                                   PLURAL NOUN

find Luke Skywalker, he is also cuter than a/an _____!
                                                    NOUN

From STAR WARS: THE FORCE AWAKENS MAD LIBS® • © & TM 2016 Lucasfilm Ltd.
Published by Price Stern Sloan, an imprint of Penguin Random House LLC, 345 Hudson Street, New York, NY 10014.

MAD LIBS® is fun to play with friends, but you can also play it by yourself! To begin with, DO NOT look at the story on the page below. Fill in the blanks on this page with the words called for. Then, using the words you have selected, fill in the blank spaces in the story.

Now you've created your own hilarious MAD LIBS® game!

# THE RULES OF BEING A JEDI KNIGHT

ADJECTIVE _____

ARTICLE OF CLOTHING (PLURAL) _____

ADJECTIVE _____

NOUN _____

VERB _____

VERB ENDING IN "ING" _____

PLURAL NOUN _____

ADJECTIVE _____

ADJECTIVE _____

NOUN _____

ADJECTIVE _____

ADVERB _____

NOUN _____

# MAD LIBS®
# THE RULES OF BEING
# A JEDI KNIGHT

Being a Jedi Knight isn't all about wearing _____
ADJECTIVE

_____ and swinging a/an _____
ARTICLE OF CLOTHING (PLURAL)                              ADJECTIVE

lightsaber around the galaxy. No, being a Jedi requires years of

_____ and discipline. To become a Jedi, you must first
NOUN

become a Padawan, which means you _____ another Jedi.
VERB

During this time, you will learn the ways of the Force, probably

_____ objects in the air and even controlling the
VERB ENDING IN "ING"

_____ of others. But be careful! During training it's easy
PLURAL NOUN

to fall to the _____ side of the Force. Then you'll become
ADJECTIVE

a/an _____ agent of _____. Once you pass a few
ADJECTIVE                    NOUN

_____ tests, you will _____ earn the honor of
ADJECTIVE                       ADVERB

being called a Jedi _____.
NOUN

From STAR WARS: THE FORCE AWAKENS MAD LIBS® • © & TM 2016 Lucasfilm Ltd.
Published by Price Stern Sloan, an imprint of Penguin Random House LLC, 345 Hudson Street, New York, NY 10014.

MAD LIBS® is fun to play with friends, but you can also play it by yourself! To begin with, DO NOT look at the story on the page below. Fill in the blanks on this page with the words called for. Then, using the words you have selected, fill in the blank spaces in the story.

Now you've created your own hilarious MAD LIBS® game!

## VACATION GUIDE TO JAKKU

ADJECTIVE _____

PERSON IN ROOM _____

ADJECTIVE _____

NOUN _____

NOUN _____

VERB _____

NOUN _____

NOUN _____

ANIMAL _____

NOUN _____

ADJECTIVE _____

VERB _____

CELEBRITY _____

# MAD LIBS

# VACATION GUIDE TO JAKKU

I see you've decided to spend your _____ vacation on Jakku.
ADJECTIVE

I'm sure _____ told you that you were _____ for
PERSON IN ROOM          ADJECTIVE

going there. After all, most people think it's a lonely _____
NOUN

floating in the Western Reaches. However, the desert _____
NOUN

of Jakku offers more than you might _____. You like
VERB

beaches, right? Well, bring your bucket and _____. Jakku
NOUN

has so much sand that the whole _____ is a beach! Also,
NOUN

it's very quiet. Look left, look right. There won't be a rancor or a/an

_____ in sight! Bring a book or _____ to pass the
ANIMAL         NOUN

time. Sure, there are lots of mines and a few _____ Star
ADJECTIVE

Destroyers here and there, but _____ past all that and come
VERB

to Jakku. You and _____ will love it!
CELEBRITY

From STAR WARS: THE FORCE AWAKENS MAD LIBS® • © & TM 2016 Lucasfilm Ltd.
Published by Price Stern Sloan, an imprint of Penguin Random House LLC, 345 Hudson Street, New York, NY 10014.

MAD LIBS® is fun to play with friends, but you can also play it by yourself! To begin with, DO NOT look at the story on the page below. Fill in the blanks on this page with the words called for. Then, using the words you have selected, fill in the blank spaces in the story.

Now you've created your own hilarious MAD LIBS® game!

# HAN AND CHEWIE: A HISTORY

ADJECTIVE _____

NOUN _____

PLURAL NOUN _____

SILLY WORD _____

NUMBER _____

ANIMAL _____

ADJECTIVE _____

ANIMAL _____

OCCUPATION _____

ADJECTIVE _____

VERB _____

ADVERB _____

NOUN _____

NOUN _____

NOUN _____

VERB _____

# MAD LIBS®
# HAN AND CHEWIE: A HISTORY

The friendship between Han Solo and Chewbacca goes back

a/an _____ time. Soon after the rise of the Empire, Han
     ADJECTIVE

saved Chewbacca, and the Wookiee swore his _____ to
                                          NOUN

Solo. They've been _____ ever since. Sometimes called
                    PLURAL NOUN

"_____," Chewbacca is the _____-foot-tall pile
 SILLY WORD                           NUMBER

of fur who sounds like a wailing _____. Han Solo is the
                                 ANIMAL

_____ smuggler who flies the *Millennium* _____
  ADJECTIVE                                  ANIMAL

and later becomes a/an _____ in the Rebel Alliance.
                    OCCUPATION

When Chewie is hit by _____ fire, Han picks up Chewie's
                 ADJECTIVE

bowcaster to _____ all their enemies. When Kylo Ren
            VERB

_____ kills Han with his _____, Chewie lets out
  ADVERB                       NOUN

a/an _____ heard all the way to the Outer Rim. Despite
     NOUN

this tragic _____, Han and Chewie's friendship will
           NOUN

_____ forever.
  VERB

MAD LIBS® is fun to play with friends, but you can also play it by yourself! To begin with, DO NOT look at the story on the page below. Fill in the blanks on this page with the words called for. Then, using the words you have selected, fill in the blank spaces in the story.

Now you've created your own hilarious MAD LIBS® game!

# STORMTROOPER JOB APPLICATION

OCCUPATION _____

PLURAL NOUN _____

VERB ENDING IN "ING" _____

ADJECTIVE _____

COLOR _____

PLURAL NOUN _____

ADJECTIVE _____

PLURAL NOUN _____

NOUN _____

ADJECTIVE _____

PLURAL NOUN _____

VERB _____

ADJECTIVE _____

NOUN _____

# MAD LIBS®
# STORMTROOPER
# JOB APPLICATION

So, you want to drop your life as a/an _____ and become
                                          OCCUPATION

a stormtrooper? Well, you should know that it's not all glitz,

_____, and _____ around the galaxy. Being
   PLURAL NOUN        VERB ENDING IN "ING"

a stormtrooper is a lot of _____ work. First, you'll need a
                               ADJECTIVE

suit of armor. Most stormtroopers wear white, but some wear black,

silver, or even _____. Then, you'll need your weapon.
                    COLOR

Most stormtroopers use _____, but the stormtroopers of
                           PLURAL NOUN

the First Order use _____ artillery, flamethrowers, and
                        ADJECTIVE

_____. After you have your _____, you must
   PLURAL NOUN                          NOUN

master it. It is essential to have _____ aim when you're
                                       ADJECTIVE

protecting your _____! If you think you're up for the
                   PLURAL NOUN

task, it's time to _____ your boring life behind. Welcome
                       VERB

to the _____ world of the First Order, _____ of
          ADJECTIVE                                  NOUN

stormtroopers!

From STAR WARS: THE FORCE AWAKENS MAD LIBS® • © & TM 2016 Lucasfilm Ltd.
Published by Price Stern Sloan, an imprint of Penguin Random House LLC, 345 Hudson Street, New York, NY 10014.

MAD LIBS® is fun to play with friends, but you can also play it by yourself! To begin with, DO NOT look at the story on the page below. Fill in the blanks on this page with the words called for. Then, using the words you have selected, fill in the blank spaces in the story.

Now you've created your own hilarious MAD LIBS® game!

# THE *MILLENNIUM FALCON,* AN OWNER'S MANUAL

VERB ENDING IN "ING" _____

NUMBER _____

ADVERB _____

ADJECTIVE _____

PLURAL NOUN _____

A PLACE _____

ADJECTIVE _____

ADJECTIVE _____

ADVERB _____

PART OF THE BODY _____

ANIMAL _____

NOUN _____

# MAD LIBS®
# THE *MILLENNIUM FALCON,*
# AN OWNER'S MANUAL

Congratulations on _____ the *Millennium Falcon*, the
<u>VERB ENDING IN "ING"</u>

ship that did the Kessel Run in only _____ parsecs. Here are
<u>NUMBER</u>

a few things you need to know:

- The ship is _____ equipped with a few modifications,
  <u>ADVERB</u>

  including a/an _____ hyperdrive and secret compartments
  <u>ADJECTIVE</u>

  where you can hide anything from droids to _____!
  <u>PLURAL NOUN</u>

- The cockpit seats four, so if there are any more passengers, they have

  to sit in (the) _____.
  <u>A PLACE</u>

- It also has two quad-laser turrets to blast those _____
  <u>ADJECTIVE</u>

  TIE fighters out of the sky.

- Spacious on the inside, yet _____ enough to
  <u>ADJECTIVE</u>

  _____ fit inside the Death Star or the _____ of
  <u>ADVERB</u>        <u>PART OF THE BODY</u>

  a giant space slug, the *Millennium* _____ is the spacecraft
  <u>ANIMAL</u>

  for you.

Fly her in good _____!
<u>NOUN</u>

From STAR WARS: THE FORCE AWAKENS MAD LIBS® • © & TM 2016 Lucasfilm Ltd.
Published by Price Stern Sloan, an imprint of Penguin Random House LLC, 345 Hudson Street, New York, NY 10014.

MAD LIBS® is fun to play with friends, but you can also play it by yourself! To begin with, DO NOT look at the story on the page below. Fill in the blanks on this page with the words called for. Then, using the words you have selected, fill in the blank spaces in the story.

Now you've created your own hilarious MAD LIBS® game!

# COME ON DOWN TO UNKAR PLUTT'S JUNK SHOP!

VERB ENDING IN "ING" _____

ADJECTIVE _____

VERB _____

ADJECTIVE _____

NUMBER _____

PERSON IN ROOM (FEMALE) _____

ADJECTIVE _____

ADJECTIVE _____

NOUN _____

TYPE OF LIQUID _____

VEHICLE _____

PLURAL NOUN _____

NOUN _____

NOUN _____

# MAD LIBS®
## COME ON DOWN TO
## UNKAR PLUTT'S JUNK SHOP!

If you've been _____ a crashed starship or a/an
<br>VERB ENDING IN "ING"

_____ Imperial Walker near Niima Outpost, you may
<br>ADJECTIVE

want to _____ your parts at the Junk Shop, owned and
<br>VERB

operated by the _____ Unkar Plutt. You can be sure to get
<br>ADJECTIVE

at least _____ times your items' value, for sure! Just last
<br>NUMBER

week, a young woman named _____ brought in a/an
<br>PERSON IN ROOM (FEMALE)

_____ gear and was paid a one-quarter portion! Okay, that's
<br>ADJECTIVE

not a lot, but it was a very _____ gear. And if you bring in
<br>ADJECTIVE

a/an _____, Unkar might pay you up to sixty portions!
<br>NOUN

When you're here, be sure to drink _____ from the well
<br>TYPE OF LIQUID

and have a look at the _____ in the back. That Corellian
<br>VEHICLE

freighter once did the Kessel Run in twelve _____! So if
<br>PLURAL NOUN

you're on Jakku, don't be a/an _____. Stop by Unkar Plutt's
<br>NOUN

_____ Shop!
<br>NOUN

From STAR WARS: THE FORCE AWAKENS MAD LIBS® • © & TM 2016 Lucasfilm Ltd.
Published by Price Stern Sloan, an imprint of Penguin Random House LLC, 345 Hudson Street, New York, NY 10014.

MAD LIBS® is fun to play with friends, but you can also play it by yourself! To begin with, DO NOT look at the story on the page below. Fill in the blanks on this page with the words called for. Then, using the words you have selected, fill in the blank spaces in the story.

Now you've created your own hilarious MAD LIBS® game!

# IF YOU SEE REY . . .

ADJECTIVE _____

A PLACE _____

COLOR _____

NOUN _____

ADJECTIVE _____

NOUN _____

NOUN _____

VERB _____

VERB ENDING IN "ING" _____

SILLY WORD _____

NUMBER _____

# MAD☺LIBS®

# IF YOU SEE REY …

**Missing:** _____ girl named Rey.
ADJECTIVE

Last seen on the surface of Jakku near (the) _____.
A PLACE

Wears plain, _____ clothing with a leather
COLOR

_____ and boots.
NOUN

**Last known residence:** The underbelly of a/an _____
ADJECTIVE

_____.
NOUN

She carries a long _____ for self-defense and knows how to
NOUN

_____ it!
VERB

**Occupation:** Scavenger, but she's also good at _____.
VERB ENDING IN "ING"

**Known friends:** None, but she does hang out with a droid named

_____.
SILLY WORD

If you know Rey's whereabouts, call 1-800-FIRST-ORDER.

**Reward:** _____ credits.
NUMBER

From STAR WARS: THE FORCE AWAKENS MAD LIBS® • © & TM 2016 Lucasfilm Ltd.
Published by Price Stern Sloan, an imprint of Penguin Random House LLC, 345 Hudson Street, New York, NY 10014.

MAD LIBS® is fun to play with friends, but you can also play it by yourself! To begin with, DO NOT look at the story on the page below. Fill in the blanks on this page with the words called for. Then, using the words you have selected, fill in the blank spaces in the story.

Now you've created your own hilarious MAD LIBS® game!

# A TOUR OF
# STARKILLER BASE

NOUN _____

VERB _____

ADVERB _____

NOUN _____

ADVERB _____

ADJECTIVE _____

VERB ENDING IN "ING" _____

ADJECTIVE _____

VERB ENDING IN "ING" _____

OCCUPATION _____

VERB _____

NOUN _____

PLURAL NOUN _____

COLOR _____

VERB ENDING IN "ING" _____

VERB _____

CELEBRITY _____

NOUN _____

# MAD LIBS
# A TOUR OF
# STARKILLER BASE

Welcome to Starkiller _____! If you haven't been here
<u>NOUN</u>

before, _____ not. It's _____ more welcoming
<u>VERB</u>       <u>ADVERB</u>

than it seems. If you thought the Death _____ was
<u>NOUN</u>

powerful . . . well, this one is _____ better. Home to the
<u>ADVERB</u>

First Order, Starkiller Base used to be a/an _____ ice planet
<u>ADJECTIVE</u>

_____ in the Unknown Regions. Now, it is the most
<u>VERB ENDING IN "ING"</u>

_____ weapon in the galaxy. Capable of _____
<u>ADJECTIVE</u>       <u>VERB ENDING IN "ING"</u>

entire star systems, the _____ of Starkiller Base can
<u>OCCUPATION</u>

pick and choose which targets to _____ (all from
<u>VERB</u>

the comfort of his or her _____). The Starkiller
<u>NOUN</u>

draws _____ from nearby stars and shoots
<u>PLURAL NOUN</u>

a/an _____ beam of such force, you're gone before
<u>COLOR</u>

you know it! So if you're interested in _____ the New
<u>VERB ENDING IN "ING"</u>

Republic (or if you just want to _____), talk to General
<u>VERB</u>

_____ and give Starkiller Base a/an _____!
<u>CELEBRITY</u>       <u>NOUN</u>

From STAR WARS: THE FORCE AWAKENS MAD LIBS® • © & TM 2016 Lucasfilm Ltd.
Published by Price Stern Sloan, an imprint of Penguin Random House LLC, 345 Hudson Street, New York, NY 10014.

MAD LIBS® is fun to play with friends, but you can also play it by yourself! To begin with, DO NOT look at the story on the page below. Fill in the blanks on this page with the words called for. Then, using the words you have selected, fill in the blank spaces in the story.

Now you've created your own hilarious MAD LIBS® game!

# YOUR LIGHTSABER AND YOU

VERB _____

ADJECTIVE _____

ADJECTIVE _____

ADVERB _____

VERB _____

COLOR _____

CELEBRITY _____

VERB _____

ADVERB _____

PLURAL NOUN _____

VERB _____

ADJECTIVE _____

NOUN _____

ADJECTIVE _____

ADJECTIVE _____

# MAD LIBS®

# YOUR LIGHTSABER AND YOU

All Jedi Knights must _____ their own lightsabers. Start
                              VERB

with the _____ hilt. Be sure it looks really _____!
            ADJECTIVE                                      ADJECTIVE

Then, _____ insert your kyber crystal and emitter matrix.
          ADVERB

But be careful, or your lightsaber could explode and _____
                                                          VERB

everyone around you! Lightsabers come in every color, including

_____. In fact, that's the color _____ has! Of
     COLOR                                        CELEBRITY

course, a lightsaber is used for combat, but it can also be used to

_____ blaster bolts, sometimes _____ reflecting
     VERB                                        ADVERB

them back at your _____. A lightsaber can also be used to
                      PLURAL NOUN

_____ through anything from _____ tauntaun
     VERB                                    ADJECTIVE

bellies to blaster doors. Once you master your lightsaber, you will

become an unstoppable _____ and strike _____
                            NOUN                          ADJECTIVE

fear into your foes. As Obi-Wan Kenobi once said about the lightsaber,

"Not as clumsy or random as a blaster. An elegant weapon for a

more _____ age."
         ADJECTIVE

From STAR WARS: THE FORCE AWAKENS MAD LIBS® • © & TM 2016 Lucasfilm Ltd.
Published by Price Stern Sloan, an imprint of Penguin Random House LLC, 345 Hudson Street, New York, NY 10014.

MAD LIBS® is fun to play with friends, but you can also play it by yourself! To begin with, DO NOT look at the story on the page below. Fill in the blanks on this page with the words called for. Then, using the words you have selected, fill in the blank spaces in the story.

Now you've created your own hilarious MAD LIBS® game!

# FINN'S DARING ESCAPE!

OCCUPATION _____

VERB _____

ARTICLE OF CLOTHING _____

NOUN _____

OCCUPATION _____

VERB _____

VERB (PAST TENSE) _____

NOUN _____

VERB _____

NOUN _____

PLURAL NOUN _____

NOUN _____

ADJECTIVE _____

ADVERB _____

ARTICLE OF CLOTHING _____

ADJECTIVE _____

# MAD LIBS

# FINN'S DARING ESCAPE!

Finn was raised to be a/an _____, but the problem
                          OCCUPATION
was that he had nothing to _____ for. So he removed
                              VERB
his _____ and ran off. Instead of turning in his
   ARTICLE OF CLOTHING
_____ to Captain Phasma, he rescued Poe, a Resistance
   NOUN
_____. After all, Poe said, "I can _____ anything!"
  OCCUPATION                                    VERB
The two men _____ a TIE fighter, but it was still attached
            VERB (PAST TENSE)
to the ship by a/an _____! Finn used the weapons to
                        NOUN
_____ the stormtroopers until Poe pulled away. Fearful of
   VERB
the tractor _____, they shot out the array under the Star
               NOUN
Destroyer. General Hux had no choice but to fire _____!
                                                  PLURAL NOUN
Since TIE fighters don't have a/an _____, Finn and Poe fled
                                      NOUN
to Jakku's _____ surface. But they were hit on the way! Finn
            ADJECTIVE
ejected and _____ parachuted down to the planet below.
               ADVERB
He took Poe's _____ and walked to the nearby town.
             ARTICLE OF CLOTHING
What's next for these two _____ heroes?
                            ADJECTIVE

MAD LIBS® is fun to play with friends, but you can also play it by yourself! To begin with, DO NOT look at the story on the page below. Fill in the blanks on this page with the words called for. Then, using the words you have selected, fill in the blank spaces in the story.

Now you've created your own hilarious MAD LIBS® game!

---

# WHY THE X-WING IS BETTER THAN THE TIE FIGHTER

ADJECTIVE _____

NOUN _____

ADJECTIVE _____

ADJECTIVE _____

ADJECTIVE _____

ADVERB _____

PLURAL NOUN _____

ADJECTIVE _____

VERB _____

NOUN _____

NOUN _____

PLURAL NOUN _____

ADJECTIVE _____

VERB _____

ADJECTIVE _____

ADJECTIVE _____

NOUN _____

VERB _____

# MAD LIBS
# WHY THE X-WING IS BETTER THAN THE TIE FIGHTER

It is _____ knowledge that the X-wing is a better
            ADJECTIVE

_____ than the TIE fighter. The most _____
        NOUN                                              ADJECTIVE

reason is that the X-wing has more firepower. Equipped with

_____ blasters and _____ torpedoes, the X-wing
     ADJECTIVE                    ADJECTIVE

_____ turns those TIE fighters into _____.
     ADVERB                                          PLURAL NOUN

Unlike the TIE fighter, the X-wing can also go into hyperspace.

If you're in a/an _____ battle and have to _____
                      ADJECTIVE                              VERB

to Dagobah to meet a new _____, the X-wing is the
                                 NOUN

_____ for you. In addition, X-wing _____ have
     NOUN                                          PLURAL NOUN

the benefit of an astromech unit. These _____ droids help
                                             ADJECTIVE

pilot the X-wing as well as _____ small repairs. Plus those
                                 VERB

_____ little droids are so cute! But the most _____
     ADJECTIVE                                               ADJECTIVE

reason the X-wing is better than the TIE _____ is that it
                                              NOUN

has shields. It's better to _____ again another day than to
                                VERB

become space debris!

MAD LIBS® is fun to play with friends, but you can also play it by yourself! To begin with, DO NOT look at the story on the page below. Fill in the blanks on this page with the words called for. Then, using the words you have selected, fill in the blank spaces in the story.

Now you've created your own hilarious MAD LIBS® game!

# MAZ KANATA AND HER LOVELY CASTLE

VERB _____

PLURAL NOUN _____

PLURAL NOUN _____

OCCUPATION _____

TYPE OF FOOD _____

ADJECTIVE _____

VERB _____

NUMBER _____

ADJECTIVE _____

PART OF THE BODY (PLURAL) _____

A PLACE _____

ADJECTIVE _____

PLURAL NOUN _____

NOUN _____

PART OF THE BODY (PLURAL) _____

PART OF THE BODY (PLURAL) _____

If you need someplace to hide or just to _____, consider
                                            VERB

Maz Kanata's castle. Nestled in the lush _____ of Takodana,
                                            PLURAL NOUN

Maz's castle can offer you rest, relaxation, and _____. Maz
                                                    PLURAL NOUN

welcomes the pirate and the _____ alike. You can eat a dish
                              OCCUPATION

of _____ at the bar, enjoy the _____ music, or
   TYPE OF FOOD                          ADJECTIVE

_____ through the jungle. Everything is great at Maz's. Maz
  VERB

herself is over _____ years old and wears _____
                  NUMBER                              ADJECTIVE

glasses that make her _____ look huge! Beware of
                        PART OF THE BODY (PLURAL)

the tunnels beneath (the) _____. _____ twists
                            A PLACE            ADJECTIVE

and turns await you, hiding many strange _____. You may
                                            PLURAL NOUN

even find a lightsaber or a/an _____! Don't expect any
                                 NOUN

privacy, though. Even the walls have _____. Most
                                       PART OF THE BODY (PLURAL)

importantly, kick up your _____ and enjoy!
                            PART OF THE BODY (PLURAL)

From STAR WARS: THE FORCE AWAKENS MAD LIBS® • © & TM 2016 Lucasfilm Ltd.
Published by Price Stern Sloan, an imprint of Penguin Random House LLC, 345 Hudson Street, New York, NY 10014.

MAD LIBS® is fun to play with friends, but you can also play it by yourself! To begin with, DO NOT look at the story on the page below. Fill in the blanks on this page with the words called for. Then, using the words you have selected, fill in the blank spaces in the story.

Now you've created your own hilarious MAD LIBS® game!

# THE CARE AND FEEDING OF YOUR RATHTAR

ADJECTIVE _____

VERB _____

ANIMAL _____

NUMBER _____

VERB _____

PLURAL NOUN _____

VERB _____

PART OF THE BODY (PLURAL) _____

PLURAL NOUN _____

VERB _____

VERB _____

ARTICLE OF CLOTHING _____

NOUN _____

OCCUPATION _____

VERB _____

# MAD☺LIBS®
# THE CARE AND FEEDING OF YOUR RATHTAR

If you're going to have a rathtar as a/an _____ pet, you should
ADJECTIVE

first _____ a few things. The rathtar is a large creature the
VERB

size of a/an _____. It has _____ rows of teeth that it
ANIMAL              NUMBER

uses to _____ anything that comes near it. Able to burst
VERB

through solid steel or even _____, rathtars are very strong.
PLURAL NOUN

They're also always hungry. Rathtars _____ anything
VERB

they can stick into their _____! If you think about
PART OF THE BODY (PLURAL)

running away, know that the rathtar has long _____ it
PLURAL NOUN

uses to _____ its prey. Even though it's huge, the rathtar
VERB

can _____ very quickly. So be sure to wear your running
VERB

_____! On second _____, maybe it's best to
ARTICLE OF CLOTHING        NOUN

leave rathtar ownership to the best _____ you know. You
OCCUPATION

can drop by any time to _____ it!
VERB

MAD LIBS® is fun to play with friends, but you can also play it by yourself! To begin with, DO NOT look at the story on the page below. Fill in the blanks on this page with the words called for. Then, using the words you have selected, fill in the blank spaces in the story.

Now you've created your own hilarious MAD LIBS® game!

# CAPTAIN PHASMA'S BIO

PLURAL NOUN _____

VERB _____

PART OF THE BODY _____

COLOR _____

ARTICLE OF CLOTHING _____

NOUN _____

VERB (PAST TENSE) _____

VERB _____

ADJECTIVE _____

PLURAL NOUN _____

VERB _____

VERB _____

# MAD LIBS

# CAPTAIN PHASMA'S BIO

Most stormtroopers are _____ who just follow orders and
PLURAL NOUN

_____. Captain Phasma, on the other _____,
VERB                                          PART OF THE BODY

is just the opposite. You can recognize Captain Phasma pretty easily

because her armor is _____, rather than white. She also
COLOR

wears a/an _____ and marches around like she owns
ARTICLE OF CLOTHING

the place. That's because Captain Phasma is in charge of all other

stormtroopers in the First Order. In fact, she knows every one by

their serial _____. Captain Phasma ran into a bit of trouble
NOUN

when Chewbacca _____ her. Chewbacca, Han Solo, and
VERB (PAST TENSE)

Finn made her _____ the shields of Starkiller Base. Then,
VERB

they threw her into the trash compactor, where she probably landed

in a pile of _____ _____. No doubt we will
ADJECTIVE          PLURAL NOUN

_____ more of Captain Phasma. It takes more than garbage
VERB

to _____ her!
VERB

From STAR WARS: THE FORCE AWAKENS MAD LIBS® • © & TM 2016 Lucasfilm Ltd.
Published by Price Stern Sloan, an imprint of Penguin Random House LLC, 345 Hudson Street, New York, NY 10014.

MAD LIBS® is fun to play with friends, but you can also play it by yourself! To begin with, DO NOT look at the story on the page below. Fill in the blanks on this page with the words called for. Then, using the words you have selected, fill in the blank spaces in the story.

Now you've created your own hilarious MAD LIBS® game!

# WHAT IS THE FORCE?

A PLACE _____

VERB _____

NOUN _____

PLURAL NOUN _____

NOUN _____

PLURAL NOUN _____

ADVERB _____

VERB _____

NOUN _____

VERB _____

VERB _____

NOUN _____

PART OF THE BODY _____

NOUN _____

VERB ENDING IN "ING" _____

A PLACE _____

SILLY WORD _____

# MAD LIBS

# WHAT IS THE FORCE?

Although the Force has not been felt in (the) _____ for
                                              A PLACE

years, it has awakened. So you should _____ a little about
                                           VERB

what it can do. The Force is an energy _____ surrounding
                                            NOUN

all living _____. It surrounds us and penetrates us—it
            PLURAL NOUN

binds the _____ together. Jedi can lift _____
              NOUN                                   PLURAL NOUN

with their minds, and can _____ sense if someone is
                              ADVERB

about to _____ them. They can also use the Jedi mind
            VERB

_____, which allows them to _____ the thoughts
    NOUN                                   VERB

of others. Some Jedi can even _____ the future! Users of
                                   VERB

the dark side of the _____ can shoot lightning from their
                          NOUN

_____. Although many people doubt the _____
PART OF THE BODY                                      NOUN

of the Force, you'd have trouble _____ if a Jedi was lifting
                                  VERB ENDING IN "ING"

you into (the) _____ and making you say " _____."
                A PLACE                                SILLY WORD

From STAR WARS: THE FORCE AWAKENS MAD LIBS® • © & TM 2016 Lucasfilm Ltd.
Published by Price Stern Sloan, an imprint of Penguin Random House LLC, 345 Hudson Street, New York, NY 10014.

MAD LIBS® is fun to play with friends, but you can also play it by yourself! To begin with, DO NOT look at the story on the page below. Fill in the blanks on this page with the words called for. Then, using the words you have selected, fill in the blank spaces in the story.

Now you've created your own hilarious MAD LIBS® game!

# WHY THE TIE FIGHTER IS BETTER THAN THE X-WING

ADJECTIVE _____

NOUN _____

COLOR _____

NUMBER _____

ADJECTIVE _____

ADJECTIVE _____

VERB _____

NUMBER _____

VERB ENDING IN "ING" _____

PLURAL NOUN _____

ADJECTIVE _____

ADJECTIVE _____

COLOR _____

ADJECTIVE _____

NOUN _____

# WHY THE TIE FIGHTER IS BETTER THAN THE X-WING

Most people agree that TIE fighters are not as _____ as
ADJECTIVE

X-wings, but there is a reason the First Order has continued to fly

them since the _____ of the Galactic Empire. The First
NOUN

Order TIE fighter has _____ wings instead of black, and
COLOR

seats _____ instead of one. TIE fighters are faster and more
NUMBER

_____ than the _____ ships the New Republic
ADJECTIVE        ADJECTIVE

uses. They are also cheaper to _____. The First Order would
VERB

rather have _____ TIE fighters than one T-70 X-wing.
NUMBER

That's why you see them _____ in _____.
VERB ENDING IN "ING"     PLURAL NOUN

TIE fighters are like swarms of _____ insects. TIE fighters
ADJECTIVE

are also solar powered. Who knew the First Order was so concerned

about the _____ environment? So if you're a stormtrooper in
ADJECTIVE

a/an _____ helmet, have no fear. The _____ First
COLOR             ADJECTIVE

Order TIE fighter will get the _____ done!
NOUN

From STAR WARS: THE FORCE AWAKENS MAD LIBS® • © & TM 2016 Lucasfilm Ltd.
Published by Price Stern Sloan, an imprint of Penguin Random House LLC, 345 Hudson Street, New York, NY 10014.

MAD LIBS® is fun to play with friends, but you can also play it by yourself! To begin with, DO NOT look at the story on the page below. Fill in the blanks on this page with the words called for. Then, using the words you have selected, fill in the blank spaces in the story.

Now you've created your own hilarious MAD LIBS® game!

# R2-D2 AND C-3PO

ADJECTIVE _____

COLOR _____

ADJECTIVE _____

VERB ENDING IN "ING" _____

FIRST NAME (FEMALE) _____

ADJECTIVE _____

NOUN _____

NOUN _____

VERB _____

NOUN _____

NOUN _____

NOUN _____

ADJECTIVE _____

SILLY WORD _____

# MAD LIBS®

# R2-D2 AND C-3PO

R2-D2 and C-3PO have been buddies for many _____
_____ADJECTIVE_____

years. Not much has changed with these two droids except for C-3PO's

_____ arm and the fact that R2-D2 has been _____
_____COLOR_____                                        _____ADJECTIVE_____

since Luke disappeared. No one quite knows why R2-D2 has been

_____. However, we do know that C-3PO has been
VERB ENDING IN "ING"

helping General _____, and R2-D2 has been hiding
_____FIRST NAME (FEMALE)_____

a/an _____ _____ in his memory banks. Soon
_____ADJECTIVE_____   _____NOUN_____

BB-8 is going to bring the missing _____ to the Resistance,
_____NOUN_____

R2-D2 will awaken, and they will _____ the two
_____VERB_____

maps together. Finally, they will know the location of Luke

_____-walker! It's a rare _____ that can last
_____NOUN_____                      _____NOUN_____

so many years, but R2-D2 and C-3PO's _____ is
_____NOUN_____

a/an _____ one! Just ask R2-D2 and he'll say, "Beep, bop,
_____ADJECTIVE_____

_____!"
_____SILLY WORD_____

From STAR WARS: THE FORCE AWAKENS MAD LIBS® • © & TM 2016 Lucasfilm Ltd.
Published by Price Stern Sloan, an imprint of Penguin Random House LLC, 345 Hudson Street, New York, NY 10014.

MAD LIBS® is fun to play with friends, but you can also play it by yourself! To begin with, DO NOT look at the story on the page below. Fill in the blanks on this page with the words called for. Then, using the words you have selected, fill in the blank spaces in the story.

Now you've created your own hilarious MAD LIBS® game!

# REY VS. KYLO REN

PART OF THE BODY _____

NOUN _____

NOUN _____

ADJECTIVE _____

NOUN _____

VERB _____

A PLACE _____

VERB ENDING IN "ING" _____

ADVERB _____

VERB _____

ADJECTIVE _____

NOUN _____

ADJECTIVE _____

NOUN _____

ADJECTIVE _____

SILLY WORD _____

NOUN _____

VERB _____

# MAD LIBS

# REY VS. KYLO REN

After Kylo Ren slices Finn right up his _____, he uses the
PART OF THE BODY

Force to summon Luke's _____ to his hand. Rey, however,
NOUN

uses her newfound _____ powers to take the lightsaber
NOUN

herself. The _____ battle that follows is the _____
ADJECTIVE                                        NOUN

of legend. They _____ through (the) _____,
VERB                            A PLACE

_____ lightsabers _____! Smoke rises. Trees
VERB ENDING IN "ING"          ADVERB

_____. Rey knows she is not as _____ as Kylo, but
VERB                              ADJECTIVE

she fights anyway. The _____ is swelling inside her. She is
NOUN

growing more and more _____ with every _____!
ADJECTIVE                        NOUN

Kylo offers to show her the _____ ways of the Force, but she
ADJECTIVE

says, "_____!" and fights on. Finally, the ground gives way
SILLY WORD

beneath them, and Rey is separated from Kylo by a/an _____.
NOUN

Rey may have won the battle, but Kylo will live to _____
VERB

another day!

MAD LIBS® is fun to play with friends, but you can also play it by yourself! To begin with, DO NOT look at the story on the page below. Fill in the blanks on this page with the words called for. Then, using the words you have selected, fill in the blank spaces in the story.

Now you've created your own hilarious MAD LIBS® game!

# LET'S FIND LUKE!

NOUN _____

PERSON IN ROOM _____

VERB _____

ADVERB _____

ANIMAL _____

A PLACE _____

NOUN _____

ADJECTIVE _____

ADJECTIVE _____

PART OF THE BODY _____

ARTICLE OF CLOTHING _____

ADJECTIVE _____

PART OF THE BODY _____

NOUN _____

VERB _____

VERB _____

# MAD LIBS

# LET'S FIND LUKE!

With Starkiller _____ destroyed, and Kylo Ren defeated
                      NOUN

by _____, there's nothing left to do but _____
      PERSON IN ROOM                                        VERB

Luke Skywalker. BB-8 and R2-D2 _____ assemble the
                                          ADVERB

map, and Chewie and Rey head out. They land the *Millennium*

_____ on an unknown world. It's a small island that looks
      ANIMAL

like (the) _____. Rey takes Luke's old _____ and
                A PLACE                                      NOUN

heads up a long flight of _____ stairs. At the top, Rey finds
                              ADJECTIVE

a/an _____ man with a robotic _____. He pulls
        ADJECTIVE                              PART OF THE BODY

off his _____ and turns around. It's Luke! Sure, he's
          ARTICLE OF CLOTHING

older. Sure, he has a big, _____ _____, but it's
                              ADJECTIVE        PART OF THE BODY

him. Rey holds out the lightsaber, and the music plays! Will Luke teach

Rey the ways of the _____? Will Finn _____ with
                          NOUN                          VERB

Chewbacca? Will R2-D2 and BB-8 compete in a "cutest droid" contest?

You'll have to _____ until the next movie to find out!
                    VERB

## Download Mad Libs today!

Join the millions of Mad Libs fans creating
wacky and wonderful stories on our apps!